# The Monarch Butterfly

PHASE 5

/ch/y/

Level 8 – Purple

# Helpful Hints for Reading at Home

The graphemes (written letters) and phonemes (units of sound) used throughout this series are aligned with Letters and Sounds. This offers a consistent approach to learning, whether reading at home or in the classroom.

**HERE IS A LIST OF PHONEMES FOR THIS PHASE OF LEARNING. AN EXAMPLE OF THE PRONUNCIATION CAN BE FOUND IN BRACKETS.**

| Phase 5 | | | |
|---|---|---|---|
| ay (day) | ou (out) | ie (tie) | ea (eat) |
| oy (boy) | ir (girl) | ue (blue) | aw (saw) |
| wh (when) | ph (photo) | ew (new) | oe (toe) |
| au (Paul) | a_e (make) | e_e (these) | i_e (like) |
| o_e (home) | u_e (rule, cube) | | |

| Phase 5 Alternative Pronunciations of Graphemes | | | |
|---|---|---|---|
| a (hat, what) | e (bed, she) | i (fin, find) | o (hot, so, other) |
| u (but, unit) | c (cat, cent) | g (got, giant) | ow (cow, blow) |
| ie (tied, field) | ea (eat, bread) | er (farmer, herb) | ch (chin, school, chef) |
| y (yes, by, very) | ou (out, shoulder, could, you) | | |

**HERE ARE SOME WORDS WHICH YOUR CHILD MAY FIND TRICKY.**

| Phase 5 Tricky Words | | | |
|---|---|---|---|
| oh | their | people | Mr |
| Mrs | looked | called | asked |
| could | | | |

## TOP TIPS FOR HELPING YOUR CHILD TO READ:

• Allow children time to break down unfamiliar words into units of sound and then encourage children to string these sounds together to create the word.

• Encourage your child to point out any focus phonics when they are used.

• Read through the book more than once to grow confidence.

• Ask simple questions about the text to assess understanding.

• Encourage children to use illustrations as prompts.

**PHASE 5** /ch/y/

This book focuses on /ch/ and /y/ and the alternative pronunciations of their graphemes. It is a Purple level 8 book band.

# Can you name these insects?

Answers: ant, moth, bee, ladybird

There are a lot of different types of butterfly. One of these pretty insects is the monarch butterfly, which is easy to spot thanks to its bright wings.

Monarch butterfly

You can tell if a butterfly is a monarch butterfly by checking the patterns on its wings. Monarchs have symmetrical wings with matching black lines and white patches.

Symmetrical means that one side is exactly the same as the other side, but flipped.

Monarchs do not have wings their whole lives. A monarch starts life as a tiny egg attached to a leaf. A female monarch butterfly lays one egg at a time.

Monarch egg

Monarch eggs hatch a few days after they have been laid. They start as little caterpillars and start eating the plant they hatched on.

Caterpillars need to eat a lot before they can mature into their butterfly form. They spend a few weeks eating constantly and shedding their skin to get bigger.

Monarch caterpillars eat lots of milkweed. This plant has toxic chemicals in it that lots of animals cannot eat. By eating milkweed, caterpillars stop predators from eating them!

Milkweed

To change into a butterfly, a caterpillar attaches to a plant and turns into a chrysalis. This is a case that caterpillars stay in while their wings grow.

A monarch butterfly cannot fly right after it comes out of its chrysalis. It must wait for its damp wings to dry out.

Monarchs do not grow bigger after the chrysalis phase, but they do still have to drink nectar for energy. They get nectar from flowers.

Monarch drinking from an orchid

As nectar is runny, monarchs can suck it up with a straw-like mouth part called a proboscis. They mostly taste with their feet, which means they can taste a flower as soon as they land.

Proboscis

When it gets chilly in the winter, some monarchs in North America migrate to a hotter place. Huge numbers of them travel to exactly the same spot in Mexico.

The trip to Mexico is a bit of a mystery to insect experts. Each butterfly that migrates there has never been before but can still somehow find where to go!

©2023 BookLife Publishing Ltd.
King's Lynn, Norfolk, PE30 4LS, UK

ISBN 978-1-80505-090-2

All rights reserved. Printed in China.
A catalogue record for this book is available from the British Library.

**The Monarch Butterfly**
Written by Charis Mather
Designed by Lucy Otter

# An Introduction to BookLife Readers...

**Our Readers have been specifically created in line with the London Institute of Education's approach to book banding and are phonetically decodable and ordered to support each phase of the Letters and Sounds document.**

Each book has been created to provide the best possible reading and learning experience. Our aim is to share our love of books with children, providing both emerging readers and prolific page-turners with beautiful books that are guaranteed to provoke interest and learning, regardless of ability.

**BOOK BAND GRADED** using the Institute of Education's approach to levelling.

**PHONETICALLY DECODABLE** supporting each phase of Letters and Sounds.

**EXERCISES AND QUESTIONS** to offer reinforcement and to ascertain comprehension.

**CLEAR DESIGN** to inspire and provoke engagement, providing the reader with clear visual representations of each non-fiction topic.

**AUTHOR INSIGHT:**
**CHARIS MATHER**

Charis Mather is a children's author at BookLife Publishing who has a love for reading and writing. Her studies in linguistics and experiences working with young readers have given her a knack for writing material that suits a range of ages and skill levels. Charis is passionate about producing books that emphasise the fun in reading and is convinced that no matter how much you already know, there is always something new to learn.

This book focuses on /ch/ and /y/ and the alternative pronunciations of their graphemes. It is a Purple level 8 book band.

**Image Credits** Images are courtesy of Shutterstock.com. With thanks to Getty Images, Thinkstock Photo and iStock– Cover – ilikestudio, LedyX, Wirestock, Phatart lab. 3 – irin-k, Andrey Pavlov, Protasov AN. 4–5 – Georgi Baird, Rabbitti. 6–7 – Breck P. Kent, Sari ONeal. 8–9 – Agnieszka Bacal, ItsAngela. 10–11 – Darkdiamond67, Leena Robinson. 12–13 – Leena Robinson, Martin Leber. 14–15 – Atosan, JHVEPhoto.